flower
FAIRIES

LINDA BLACKMOOR

ISBN: 978-1-966417-11-8 (PRINT)

PUBLISHED BY QUILL PRESS. LINDA BLACKMOOR'S TITLES MAY BE PURCHASED IN BULK FOR EDUCATIONAL, BUSINESS, FUNDRAISING, OR SALES PROMOTIONAL USE. FOR INFORMATION, PLEASE EMAIL HELLO@LINDABLACKMOOR.COM

FIRST PRINT EDITION: 2025

LINDA BLACKMOOR
WWW.LINDABLACKMOOR.COM

rose

FAIRY

In a garden of roses, you may catch a glitter of wings dancing beneath the warm sun's glow. There, the Rose Fairy lovingly tends rows of enchanting blossoms—hybrid teas, joyful floribundas, daring climbers, and delicate miniatures. With a tender touch, she paints the roses in brilliant hues of fiery reds, soft pinks, pure whites, and every magical shade in between, transforming the garden into a wondrous fairy tale land. On summer days, the breeze carries their sweet fragrance into the air.

FLOWER MEANING:

Roses symbolize love, fairy-tale royalty, sparkling beauty, gentle magic, secret wishes, and enchanting mystery.

A FAIRY'S GROWING TIPS:

- Plant marigolds or sweet alyssum nearby to attract beneficial insects, offering your roses natural pest protection.
- Regular pruning sparks fresh buds and strengthens the overall plant.
- In colder climates, mound mulch or compost around the base in late fall to insulate roots.

lavender

FAIRY

In a quiet corner of the meadow, you may glimpse a delicate shimmer of wings fluttering amid tall, violet spires. There, the Lavender Fairy gently tends her fragrant fields—English lavender, sweet French varieties, and graceful Spanish blooms. With a soothing touch, she dusts the blossoms in gentle purples, soft blues, and whispers of silver, turning the meadow into a realm of calm enchantment. Come twilight, their gentle perfume drifts on the evening breeze, weaving serenity through every hushed corner of the meadow.

FLOWER MEANING:

Lavender symbolizes calming magic, gentle healing, peaceful dreams, quiet wisdom, spiritual grace, and tranquil protection.

A FAIRY'S GROWING TIPS:

- Place lavender near walkways or garden paths so the gentle brush of passing feet releases its soothing aroma into the air.
- Let the topsoil rest before watering again, keeping the roots safe from rot.
- Pinch or prune the soft tips regularly to encourage fuller fragrant blooms.

– SUNFLOWER

sunflower

FAIRY

In the heart of a sunny valley, a joyful fairy greets each morning with open arms. She is the Sunflower Fairy, caring for giant Mammoth blooms that sway in the breeze and tiny Dwarf sunflowers that smile at the sky. She helps each flower stand proud, gently turning its bright face toward the warm sun. Like a careful painter, she colors every petal in glowing yellows and soft oranges, filling the valley with happy light. Each afternoon, the gentle rustle of leaves and cheerful birdsong reflect her bright spirit far and wide.

FLOWER MEANING:

Sunflowers symbolize joyous optimism, devotion, heartfelt gratitude, radiant hope, generous warmth, and uplifting spirit.

A FAIRY'S GROWING TIPS:

- Give each seedling room to grow, as sunflowers need plenty of elbow room for strong roots and tall stems.
- For taller varieties, place stakes or supports early on to help them withstand breezes.
- After the blooms fade, let the heads mature so you can harvest seeds.

- TULIP

tulip

FAIRY

In a bright spring garden, a gentle fairy appears to welcome each new bloom. She is the Tulip Fairy, caring for tall Darwin tulips with strong stems and fancy Parrot tulips with ruffled petals. She guides their soft buds through the cool morning air, adding splashes of pink, red, yellow, and purple to the garden. Like a joyful artist, she paints every petal with hope and wonder. By midday, the tulips stand proudly under the warm sun, sharing their sweet, cheerful spirit with everyone who passes by.

FLOWER MEANING:

Tulips stand for fresh beginnings, warm affection, simple happiness, and bright hope.

A FAIRY'S GROWING TIPS:

- Tuck tulip bulbs into the ground in autumn so they can rest during winter and pop up in spring.
- Tulips like cool, well-drained soil—be careful not to overwater so their bulbs stay cozy and dry.
- Once petals fall, let the leaves soak up sunshine to feed the bulb for next year.

lily

FAIRY

In a quiet glen, a graceful fairy greets the early light. She is the Lily Fairy, caring for bright Asiatic lilies and sweetly scented Oriental lilies. She helps them unfurl their elegant petals in soft whites, pinks, and oranges, lighting the garden with gentle color. Like a caring artist, she guides each bloom to stand proud. By dusk, their sweet perfume drifts on the evening breeze, sharing calm and wonder with all who wander by.

FLOWER MEANING:

Lilies stand for gentle purity, hope, new beginnings, and a loving heart.

A FAIRY'S GROWING TIPS:

- Plant lily bulbs in early spring or fall, tucking them into well-draining soil.
- Add a little support if tall stems start to lean, using small stakes or a friendly neighbor plant.
- After the flowers fade, let the leaves soak in the sunshine so they can recharge.

- DAFFODIL

daffodil

FAIRY

In a hidden hollow, a cheerful fairy appears at the very start of spring. She is the Daffodil Fairy, guiding tall trumpets and sweet little narcissus through the last chill of winter. She helps them bloom in bright yellows and soft whites, lighting the garden with hope. Like a gentle friend, she encourages each flower to stand proud. By midday, their happy faces bob in the breeze, sharing warmth and delight with all who wander by.

FLOWER MEANING:

Daffodils bring fresh beginnings, warm friendship, and bright springtime joy.

A FAIRY'S GROWING TIPS:

- Plant bulbs in fall so they can rest through winter and pop up when the weather warms.
- Water sparingly so the bulbs stay healthy and don't get soggy.
- After the flowers fade, let the leaves soak up sunlight to feed next year's blooms.

petunia
FAIRY

In a sunny patch of the yard, a friendly fairy welcomes big, bold blooms. She is the Petunia Fairy, caring for wave petunias that trail from hanging baskets and grandiflora petunias with large, showy petals. She helps them open wide in shades of pink, purple, and white, brightening the garden with color. By midday, each blossom sways in the breeze, offering cheer and a warm welcome to all who pass by.

FLOWER MEANING:

Petunias symbolize playful color, gentle comfort, bright cheer, heartfelt acceptance, sweet encouragement, and joyful resilience.

A FAIRY'S GROWING TIPS:

- Wait until the last frost passes so tiny petunia plants can stay cozy and safe.
- Wave petunias love to spread, so give them room to roam or hang them high so they can trail down.
- Pinch off old flowers often, helping new blooms burst forth all season long.

daisy
FAIRY

In a bright meadow, a gentle fairy helps sweet daisies pop up through the soft grass. She is the Daisy Fairy, tending Shasta daisies with tall white petals and tiny English daisies that sprinkle the lawn with pinks. She guides each bloom to lift its face to the sun, bringing a playful, cheery glow to the field. By afternoon, the daisies sway in the breeze, sharing their happy dance with bees and butterflies who come to visit.

FLOWER MEANING:

Daisies stand for childlike wonder, fresh beginnings, cheerful optimism, warm friendship, simple joy, and bright innocence.

A FAIRY'S GROWING TIPS:

- Plant daisy seeds or small plants in early spring, giving them time to grow strong before the heat arrives.
- Place them in full sun so their blossoms stay bright and showy.
- Once each flower fades, gently snip it away to encourage new buds to open all season long.

peony
FAIRY

In a soft, sunny corner of the garden, a quiet fairy tends her lush blooms. She is the Peony Fairy, caring for billowy double peonies and sweet single-petal varieties. She coaxes each bud to unfurl in shades of pink, white, and red, filling the air with a gentle, powdery scent. By midday, her blossoms grow large and graceful, inviting butterflies and bees to gather and share in their calm beauty.

FLOWER MEANING:

Peonies stand for gentle prosperity, sweet blessings, quiet grace, comforting hope, warm devotion, and enduring joy.

A FAIRY'S GROWING TIPS:

- Plant peony roots in early spring or fall, giving them time to settle into cool, well-draining soil.
- Keep them in a spot with plenty of light so they can form big, beautiful blooms.
- Once blossoms fade, trim them away and let the leafy stems soak up sunlight.

lotus
FAIRY

In a still pond, a graceful fairy watches over her floating blooms. She is the Lotus Fairy, tending pink lotus buds that slowly unfold and white varieties that sparkle in the morning light. She coaxes each flower to rise from the water in a show of quiet beauty. Each morning, she welcomes new buds to greet the sun while old petals float away like tiny boats. By midday, the lily pads dance under the warm rays, sharing a calm, gentle magic with every visiting dragonfly and frog.

FLOWER MEANING:

Lotuses stand for calm reflection, gentle renewal, spiritual growth, quiet purity, hidden potential, and peaceful beginnings.

A FAIRY'S GROWING TIPS:

- Start lotus tubers in a wide container filled with rich, heavy soil, then sink it gently into still water.
- Keep the water warm and shallow at first, letting leaves reach the surface before gradually placing the pot deeper.
- Once flowers fade, remove old petals so new growth can flourish in the sun.

hydrangea
FAIRY

In a quiet corner of the yard, a gentle fairy tends her soft, puffy blooms. She is the Hydrangea Fairy, caring for bright mophead clusters and delicate lacecap flowers that shift from pink to blue. She sprinkles light morning dew to keep their colors shining and their leaves fresh. In early summer, she coaxes the buds to open, creating soft pastel clouds that dance in the breeze. By afternoon, the big blossoms glow under gentle sunlight, inviting curious bees and butterflies to stop by.

FLOWER MEANING:

Hydrangeas stand for heartfelt understanding, warm gratitude, gentle grace, friendship, honest emotions, and kindness.

A FAIRY'S GROWING TIPS:

- Plant where they can soak up morning sun but enjoy some afternoon shade.
- Water deeply during hot days to keep the blooms lush and happy.
- Add lime or soil acid to shift petals from pink to blue, creating a bit of color magic in the garden.

magnolia FAIRY

In a peaceful grove, a quiet fairy tends her majestic blooms. She is the Magnolia Fairy, caring for regal saucer magnolias and sweet star magnolias that open in shades of pink, white, and buttery cream. She gently blows morning mist over each bud, coaxing them to unfurl with graceful charm. At the first sign of spring, their blossoms fill the air with a soft, lemony fragrance. By midday, the grand flowers stretch toward the sun, welcoming gentle breezes and curious bees.

FLOWER MEANING:

Magnolias stand for quiet dignity, perseverance, timeless elegance, steadfast love, hope, and graceful beauty.

A FAIRY'S GROWING TIPS:

- Choose a sunny, sheltered spot so chilly winds don't harm the tender buds.
- Spread mulch in spring to keep shallow roots cool and moist, avoiding weeds.
- Leave space around the trunk, as digging too close can damage the fragile root system.

carnation

FAIRY

Behind an ivy-draped cottage, a quiet fairy tends her ruffled treasures. She is the Carnation Fairy, delighting in the bold colors of Grenadin carnations and the sweet scents of Chabaud varieties. At dawn, she drapes the petals with soft ribbons of dew, revealing a tapestry of pink, white, and red blooms. By midday, a gentle breeze carries their light perfume around the hidden garden, whispering tales of old. When evening settles, she gathers fallen petals as keepsakes, promising fresh blossoms in the coming day.

FLOWER MEANING:

Carnations stand for admiration, devotion, comfort, friendly warmth, gratitude, and quiet grace.

A FAIRY'S GROWING TIPS:

- Choose a spot with slightly alkaline, well-draining soil so Grenadin and Chabaud carnations can thrive.
- Water at the base and avoid soaking the leaves, helping prevent rot.
- Stake taller stems early to support the flowers' weight and keep their ruffled petals in perfect display

marigold
FAIRY

In a sunny nook by a weathered fence, a cheerful fairy tends her golden tapestry. She is the Marigold Fairy, caring for tall African marigolds with big, fluffy blooms and smaller French marigolds with bright, fiery petals. Each morning, she gently awakens the buds, urging them to open in vivid shades of yellow and orange. By midday, a peppery scent drifts across the garden, adding a spark of warmth to the air. As evening settles, she gathers a few dried blossoms, saving seeds like tiny treasures for next year's bright display.

FLOWER MEANING:

Marigolds stand for optimism, cheer, friendly protection, loving devotion, creative spirit, and vibrant celebration.

A FAIRY'S GROWING TIPS:

- Pick a sunny spot with light, well-draining soil so African and French marigolds can shine.
- Clip off old flowers to keep new buds blooming strong all season long.
- Plant marigolds near vegetables or roses to help deter common garden pests naturally.

orchid
FAIRY

In a hidden greenhouse behind a vine-laced gate, a regal fairy tends her exotic treasures. She is the Orchid Fairy, carefully watching over elegant Phalaenopsis (moth orchids) and vibrant Cattleya blooms. At sunrise, she polishes each petal, coaxing them to reveal their delicate shapes and colors. By noon, the greenhouse fills with a soft, sweet perfume, whispering secrets of these enchanting flowers. When dusk settles, she collects dewdrops from the leaves, storing them in tiny vials to nurture future blooms.

FLOWER MEANING:

Orchids stand for refined grace, rare beauty, strength, love, mystery, and unwavering admiration.

A FAIRY'S GROWING TIPS:

- Provide bright, indirect light and moderate humidity to mimic a warm, tropical home.
- Water sparingly, allowing the bark-based potting mix to dry slightly between drinks to avoid soggy roots.
- Feed with a gentle orchid fertilizer during active growth.

www.ingramcontent.com/pod-product-compliance
Lightning Source LLC
Chambersburg PA
CBHW060834270326
41933CB00002B/83